A Note From Denise Renner

The Word of God is so powerful in our lives. It is essential that every person spend time with God and study His Word in order to stay spiritually strong in these last days.

This study guide corresponds to my *TIME With Denise Renner* TV program by the same title that can be viewed at **deniserenner.org**. My desire is that through these lessons, you find the encouragement and freedom in Christ that you need. I believe the Holy Spirit is going to speak to you through the words you read in this study tool and that as you begin to use it, you will be *propelled* into the abundant life God has planned for you. I encourage you to make the effort to receive all He has for you and all He wants to do in you — it will definitely be worth it!

Whether you have walked with the Lord a long time or have just begun to follow Him, there is so much He wants to give you from His Word. He sees where you are, and He wants to meet you there.

> Therefore do not worry about tomorrow, for tomorrow
> will worry about its own things.
> Sufficient for the day is its own trouble.
> Matthew 6:34

Your sister and friend in Jesus Christ,

Denise Renner

The Greater One on the Inside

Copyright © 2022 by Denise Renner
1814 W. Tacoma St.
Broken Arrow, Oklahoma 74012

Published by Rick Renner Ministries
www.renner.org

ISBN 13: 978-1-6675-0312-7

eBook ISBN 13: 978-1-6675-0313-4

TOPIC

There Is a Lover Inside Us — Who Is He?

SCRIPTURES

1. **1 John 4:4** — You are of God, little children, and have overcome them, because He who is in you is greater than he who is in the world.

2. **Romans 5:5** — Now hope does not disappoint, because the love of God has been poured out in our hearts by the Holy Spirit who was given to us.

3. **1 John 4:20** — If someone says, "I love God," and hates his brother, he is a liar; for he who does not love his brother whom he has seen, how can he love God whom he has not seen?

4. **1 Corinthians 13:4-8** — Love suffers long and is kind; love does not envy; love does not parade itself, is not puffed up; does not behave rudely, does not seek its own, is not provoked, thinks no evil; does not rejoice in iniquity, but rejoices in the truth; bears all things, believes all things, hopes all things, endures all things. Love never fails. But whether there are prophecies, they will fail; whether there are tongues, they will cease; whether there is knowledge, it will vanish away.

5. **Romans 8:38,39** — For I am persuaded that neither death nor life, nor angels nor principalities nor powers, nor things present nor things to come, nor height nor depth, nor any other created thing, shall be able to separate us from the love of God which is in Christ Jesus our Lord.

6. **Isaiah 41:10** — Fear not, for I am with you; Be not dismayed, for I am your God. I will strengthen you, yes, I will help you, I will uphold you with My righteous right hand.

SYNOPSIS

With the new birth comes the indwelling power and presence of the Holy Spirit. The Bible teaches that the Holy Spirit living inside the believer is greater than anyone or anything else in the world. The Holy Spirit's power can be expressed in a variety of ways, but one of the greatest attributes of His presence is the ability to love others with Christ's love. This love is supernatural and can be released at any time with the help of the Holy Spirit.

The emphasis of this lesson:

One of the most valuable benefits of the Holy Spirit living inside you is the ability to love others with the love of God. When you receive Christ in the new birth, the Holy Spirit comes to live inside you and helps you to love others with God's love. By acknowledging His presence and His role as the Greater One inside, you can release the power of the Holy Spirit into every circumstance. Your relationships will change as you begin to operate in the love of God.

The Greater One Inside

As born-again believers, we have an incredible power source inside us, and that is the Person of the Holy Spirit. In fact, the Bible refers to Him as the Greater One within us. First John 4:4 says, "You are of God, little children, and have overcome them because *He who is in you is greater* than he who is in the world."

No matter what we face around us, we can rest assured that the Holy Spirit living in us will help us live as overcomers. He is the Greater One! No circumstance is too difficult for His mighty power to change.

The Holy Spirit expresses Himself through our lives in so many powerful ways. Not only does He help us triumph over outward situations, but He also enables us to conquer enemies inside our own hearts through the development of the fruit of the Spirit in our lives. By releasing the power of the Greater One inside us, we can defeat every giant standing in our way and live an overcoming life in Christ Jesus.

The Power of God's Love

One of the most valuable benefits of the Holy Spirit living inside us is the ability to love others with the love of God. The world doesn't have this kind of love because it is the result of the Holy Spirit's inward working in our hearts. Romans 5:5 states, "Now hope does not disappoint, because *the love of God has been poured out in our hearts by the Holy Spirit* who was given to us." God's nature of love has been imparted to us through the Greater One, and that love can impact everyone we meet as we give place to it.

This supernatural impartation of the love of God happened the moment we made Jesus our Lord and Savior. When we became born again, the love of God came inside us to dwell in our hearts. It's not there for just a certain moment, week, month, or year. This supernatural love *always* resides within us! It's available for us to draw from at any moment for the rest of our lives. In fact, one of the signs of being a born-again believer is that we can love people!

Once the love of God has been imparted to us through the indwelling presence of the Holy Spirit, it changes our lives — our attitudes and our actions or behaviors, including our words. It transforms the way we think about people and causes us to pursue peace in our relationships.

In her teaching, Denise recalled how God's love changed her when she became born again. Immediately, she had a desire in her heart to love everyone! This love caused her to apologize to her mother for past arguments, and it brought peace into their relationship. She didn't want to argue with her mother anymore because she was filled with the love of God.

The love of God also causes us to be selfless and self-sacrificing. In fact, the Bible tells us that no one has greater love than to lay down his own life for his friends (*see* John 15:13). That's the kind of love Jesus demonstrated for us — He sacrificed His life for our sins. That love is powerful!

We may never lay down our physical life for another, but we can be selfless and think of others instead of just ourselves. We can give up judging others or being critical of them. We can give up jealousy and rejoice with them instead. When God's love is in us, it causes us to let go of our selfish ways and to be considerate of other people.

Whenever we're tempted to act ugly or unkind toward another, we can remember that the Greater One lives inside us to help us in our weaknesses. Then we can draw from that power deep inside us and release the supernatural love of God to others. If someone treats us unfairly, we can remind ourselves that God's love is inside us. We can forgive people regardless of what they might have done. That kind of power comes from the Holy Spirit and is an expression of the love of God.

God's love can conquer any negative emotion that may try to bubble up in our hearts. It can conquer jealousy, criticism, and fear. It can even overcome the temptation to gossip!

To help us understand the magnitude of God's love living inside us, the Bible outlines specific attributes of this kind of love. The truth from God's Word shines a light on areas that we need to correct or adjust. Because it is a lamp unto our feet and a light unto our path, God's Word will guide us in loving others properly. When trials and temptations come and we don't know how to deal with certain situations, the Bible shows us exactly what to do and how to express God's love correctly — even when our flesh is tempted to do otherwise.

For example, First John 4:20 says, "If someone says, 'I love God,' and hates his brother, he is a liar; for he who does not love his brother whom he has seen, how can he love God whom he has not seen?" This verse corrects us whenever we find it difficult to love others, including our natural relatives — and even our brothers and sisters in Christ! It shines a light on our path and reveals to us an area that may need to be corrected if we're not walking in the love of God properly.

Sometimes we can encounter sensitive or complicated situations with people that make walking in love difficult. However, by taking hold of the Word of God, we can receive the wisdom we need — the light that illuminates our path — to show us how to proceed. We can then activate the conquering power of God's love by releasing it from our hearts in obedience to His Word.

Jesus said there were two great commandments — to love Him with all our heart, soul, and mind, and to love our neighbor as ourselves (*see* Matthew 22:37-39). These are not just casual suggestions; they are commandments for us to draw upon the love of God that's been shed abroad in our hearts by the Holy Ghost when we became born again. When we love Him with our whole heart, soul, and mind, and love our neighbor as we love ourselves, we are acknowledging the Greater One on the inside who expresses Himself through the love of God.

God raised the standard when it comes to loving others. In fact, when Peter asked Jesus how many times a person should forgive his brother in a day, Jesus' reply was, "…Seventy times seven" (Matthew 18:22). That's 490 times! Only the God-kind of love has the strength and power to forgive someone that many times in a single day.

God's Love Is Ready To Operate Through You

Here's the magnificent news — God's love is in you, and it's ready to operate. It's immediately available to empower you to release forgiveness. It is ready to help you stop gossiping. It is there for you to believe the best of every person, to stop criticizing others, and to have patience with people. Because God's love is already inside you, all you need to do is acknowledge its power and release it by faith.

You may not feel like loving a certain person right now, but you can love that person because you've been made the righteousness of God. You can step out in faith and forgive someone even if your mind doesn't agree. You can choose to operate in the love of God because it's already inside you by the power and presence of the Holy Ghost.

If you're not sure what God's love would do in a situation, just go back to the Word of God. It will show you what love looks like and how it operates. As you look into the perfect law of liberty (*see* James 1:25), the Holy Spirit will quicken your heart and show you how to release His love into any and every circumstance.

One of the best places to learn about God's love is from First Corinthians 13 — sometimes called "the love chapter" — especially verses 4-8. This chapter describes in detail the various attributes of divine love. It shows us that love is patient, kind, doesn't envy or boast, is not provoked, and doesn't think evil. God's love doesn't rejoice in sin but rejoices in truth. It bears all things, hopes all things, and endures all things. And the most amazing thing of all — love does not fail!

The Bible also says there is no law against the love of God (*see* Galatians 5:22,23). Nothing can stand against this kind of divine love; it can never fail. And when we apply God's love in our lives, it conquers all.

Love can be likened to a garden tiller that pulls out all the weeds and makes the ground soft and ready to receive seed. Love can go into the ground of any heart and remove hate, criticism, and jealousy. It can throw out fear and gossip. Because it's the most powerful thing on this earth, God's love can triumph over anything standing in its way.

The greatest act of love was Jesus laying down His life for ours. His love brought redemption — salvation and deliverance. It freed us from the judgment and wrath of God and gave us the right to enter Heaven when we pass from this life. Now, through the new birth, Jesus' powerful love has been placed inside us by the Holy Ghost. This is a conquering kind of love!

To release love's conquering power in your life, you can simply say, "God, I agree with You. I agree that You are greater than my complicated and difficult situation. You said in Your Word that the Greater One is in me, and I look to Him now for help, strength, and power."

Remember, the Holy Spirit on the inside of you is greater than he that's in the world (*see* 1 John 4:4). He's greater than any pressure, confusion, fear, doubt, or pain. And because the Greater One is living in you, He empowers you to conquer unforgiveness, criticism, jealousy, envy, and strife. With His help, you can put down your pride and let go of the hurt and pain that others may have inflicted upon you. The love of God inside you releases forgiveness. It lets things go and doesn't hold grudges.

By allowing the love of God to operate in our lives, we're acknowledging the presence of the Greater One in us. It's impossible to be separated from Him because He came to live inside you when you received Christ and were born again. Romans 8:38 and 39 remind us: "For I am persuaded that neither death nor life, nor angels nor principalities nor powers, nor things present nor things to come, nor height nor depth, nor any other created thing, shall be able to separate us from the love of God which is in Christ Jesus our Lord." This powerful love resides in us *at all times*, and we can access it every day by faith.

Friend, you can't escape the love of God when you're born again. His love is in you always. God's presence will never leave you, and the Lord will continue to uphold you with His righteous right hand (*see* Isaiah 41:10). To activate His love that is already present within you, simply acknowledge the Holy Spirit — the Greater One. Study God's Word and discover how this love operates and acts in the daily affairs of life. Then, as you learn to release this love by faith, every circumstance around you will begin to change by the power of God's love.

STUDY QUESTIONS

Be diligent to present yourself approved to God, a worker who does not need to be ashamed, rightly dividing the word of truth.
— 2 Timothy 2:15

1. First John 4:4 says, "You are of God, little children, and have over-come them, because He who is in you is greater than he who is in the world." How does this scripture change your perspective of the challenges or circumstances surrounding you today?

2. Romans 5:5 states, "Now hope does not disappoint, because the love of God has been poured out in our hearts by the Holy Spirit who was given to us." Do you remember the first time your actions or attitudes toward others changed after you became born again?

3. First John 4:20 says, "If someone says, 'I love God,' and hates his brother, he is a liar; for he who does not love his brother whom he has seen, how can he love God whom he has not seen?" How is this verse correcting areas in your life and relationships?

PRACTICAL APPLICATION

But be doers of the word,
and not hearers only, deceiving yourselves.
—James 1:22

Release God's love by acknowledging the power and presence of the Greater One inside you.

1. In times past, how have you acknowledged the power of the Holy Spirit inside you in relation to God's love?

2. What relationship in your life is the most difficult right now? How are you releasing God's love into that relationship?

3. What testimonies have you experienced by releasing God's love? How did a situation or relationship change because you chose to acknowl-edge the Greater One inside you and operate in divine love?

TOPIC

Peace Is the Guard Over Your Heart

SCRIPTURES

1. **Philippians 4:7** (*KJV*) — And the peace of God, which passeth all understanding, shall keep your hearts and minds through Christ Jesus.
2. **Proverbs 15:1** — A soft answer turns away wrath, but a harsh word stirs up anger.
3. **Proverbs 15:28** — The heart of the righteous studies how to answer, but the mouth of the wicked pours forth evil.
4. **Proverbs 16:23,24** — The heart of the wise teaches his mouth, and adds learning to his lips. Pleasant words are like a honeycomb, sweetness to the soul and health to the bones.

SYNOPSIS

One of the magnificent ways the Holy Spirit expresses Himself is by peace. Not only is peace one of the fruits of the new life in Christ, but it also helps believers keep calm in conflict and controversy. By acknowledging the help of the Holy Spirit and allowing His peace to flow out from inside their hearts, Christians can speak peaceful words, bring peace into stressful situations, and be a blessing to others.

The emphasis of this lesson:

God's powerful peace is resident inside every believer through the indwelling presence of the Holy Spirit. By studying God's Word, you can understand how God's peace operates in the daily affairs of life. The Bible provides practical keys for walking in peace — and a lot of that has to do with what comes out of your mouth! Your words are powerful containers that can turn away wrath and impart healing into the lives of those around you.

The Power of God's Peace

Through the new birth, the Holy Spirit came to live inside us. He is the Greater One, and His power is present in our hearts. He expresses Himself through us in many wonderful ways, including through what the Bible calls the fruit of the Spirit. Let's look at another part of this special fruit —the powerful fruit of peace.

Have you ever been in a difficult, tense, or fearful situation, and all of a sudden peace just flooded your heart? From a natural standpoint, you might have had every reason to get upset, cry, or scream, but instead, you acted in a peaceful way. Isn't it wonderful when peace conquers a troubling or emotionally charged environment? That's the power of God's peace working in you!

Philippians 4:7 in the *King James Version* says, "And the peace of God, which passeth all understanding, shall *keep* your hearts and minds through Christ Jesus." The word "keep" in this verse means *to put a guard up and over* our hearts. In other words, we have to place peace as a guard against things that would try to sneak into our hearts and pollute them with toxins. We have to say, "No. Doubt you're not coming in. Fear, you're not coming in. Gossip and hate, you're not coming in." When we allow peace to stand like a guard over our hearts, we're denying access to ungodly attitudes and behaviors that would try to trip us up in our walk with God.

If you've ever visited a palace or seen pictures of one, you might have noticed guards standing outside the gates. What are they doing? They are protecting the precious people and the treasures inside that palace.

In the same manner, this is how peace works in our life. It is like a guard stationed at the gate of our heart protecting all the precious treasures inside. By giving permission to godliness and denying access to ungodliness, peace preserves the purity of our heart.

Another characteristic of God's peace is that it "passes all understanding" (Philippians 4:7). When peace is in operation, it flows from the presence of God inside us. It gives us tranquility, quietness, and calmness when natural circumstances surrounding us would otherwise make us upset, frustrated, anxious, or angry.

We may not always understand why we're able to keep our composure in certain situations, but we can rejoice because God's peace goes beyond our human reasoning or thinking. The presence of God's peace — especially in difficult situations — reveals God's magnificent power working in our lives. It is a sign of the presence of the Holy Spirit in our hearts. The fruit of peace is a remarkable expression of the Greater One inside us!

Practical Keys for Walking in God's Peace

Now that we understand that God's peace is resident inside us through the indwelling of the Holy Spirit, we must learn how to apply that peace on a daily basis. We can't just sit around wishing for peace to happen, because we are still responsible to release the power of the Greater One within us. In every situation we encounter, we must cooperate with the Holy Spirit by obeying the Word of God to bring peace into our lives.

One of the most important factors that determines our peace is our words. What comes out of our mouths can easily change the thermostat of any situation. In fact, we see an example of just how powerful peaceful words can be in Mark 4:39 when Jesus spoke to the storm and said, "Peace, be still." While His disciples were fearful of losing their lives at sea, Jesus took action with His words. He didn't stand idly by watching the wind and waves — He got up and spoke with authority to the storm. After He declared peace over the situation, the storm stopped.

In the same way, we can release God's peace into the storms of life through the words we speak, which should always come from the Word of God. It's easy to let our emotions pull us off track. Feelings of fear, anxiety, frustration, and anger are not peaceful and can easily cause us to make wrong decisions or to say things we regret. However, when we take hold of the tools of the Word of God, we can remain stable in very unstable times.

The Bible says that God's Word is a lamp unto our feet and a light unto our path (*see* Psalm 119:105). It has the power to illuminate the right path in front of us. It shows us where to place our feet so that our steps don't falter. The Word keeps us anchored and full of peace, no matter what the situation around us looks like.

One of the first instructions the Bible gives us regarding our words is found in Proverbs 15:1, which says, "A soft answer turns away wrath, but a harsh word stirs up anger." Think about that for a moment — a soft answer is more powerful than wrath. It will stop wrath in its tracks. On the contrary, a harsh word simply stirs up anger. It will only escalate a situation and make it worse.

For example, if someone falsely accuses you of something, you have a choice to respond with soft or angry words. By recognizing God's peace inside you, you can make sure that what you speak brings forth peace and de-escalates the situation. You might have to say, "Excuse me for a moment. I'll be right back. We can discuss this further, but I need a minute." You can then step away from the conversation and focus on the peace of God inside you. That's the manifested presence of the Greater One, and He wants to express Himself through peace in that situation. Once you grab hold of His peace, you can re-enter the conversation and respond with a soft answer.

At certain times in relationships, anger can be a real feeling that may come toward you. But you don't have to receive it. You can be a doer of the Word, put up your guard of peace, and say, "No. Anger, you're not coming in." And then you can respond with a soft answer, which will turn away wrath. This is how powerful God's peace operates in daily life!

Another piece of instruction God's Word gives us regarding our words comes from Proverbs 15:28, which states, "The heart of the righteous studies how to answer, but the mouth of the wicked pours forth evil." When you're involved in a sensitive or controversial discussion, you can apply God's peace by studying how to answer with truth and love. Perhaps you might need to write down what you need to say or plan out how you can respond. However you reflect upon your answer, the Bible teaches that you need to study how to answer if you want to walk in peace. Again, *your mouth* has a lot to do with the peace you experience.

If you get into a situation with a person and all you want to do is talk about it to one person after another, you're not studying how to answer. You're just stirring up your emotions. You're talking more about the problem or how that person needs to change. But when you do this, you're building up a case against that person in your heart, and it's not going to bring you peace. You need to follow God's Word and *study* how to answer. After you've prepared your response, you need to deliver it in such a way that it not only turns away wrath but also promotes truth, love, and peace.

Here's another set of instructions for how to use our words properly from Proverbs 16:23 and 24: "The heart of the wise teaches his mouth, and adds learning to his lips. Pleasant words are like a honeycomb, sweetness to the soul and health to the bones." You can apply this verse to any conversation you have — even to ones that are difficult or confrontational. Your response in a sensitive situation can bring sweetness to someone's soul and add health to their bones. That's the power of a peaceful answer!

The gospels give us several examples of how Jesus spoke words of peace that changed a situation. For example, in John chapter 8, when the woman who was caught in adultery was brought before Jesus, the religious leaders were trying to start a fight. They kept asking Jesus, "What are You going to do about her?" This was an emotionally charged situation that was escalating quickly! But instead of giving into the arguments and fighting back, Jesus gave forth a wise, peaceful answer. He wrote in the ground and then said to them, "He who is without sin among you, let him throw a stone at her first" (John 8:6,7). The Bible says that one by one, each of these religious leaders dropped their stones and walked away. To the woman caught in adultery, Jesus said, "Woman, where are your accusers? Oh, there are none. I don't accuse you either. Go and sin no more" (*see* John 8:10,11). Because Jesus expressed the peace inside Him, the situation completely changed.

Similarly, we can de-escalate situations surrounding us when we simply allow the Holy Spirit to express His peace inside our hearts. The Greater One is greater than any storm.

Perhaps things around us look bleak or hopeless. It may even appear that failure is on the horizon. But we won't sink if we keep our eyes on Jesus. He's with us in our boat! The Greater One is inside us, and He wants to express Himself through us in every situation we encounter. He wants to bring His peace!

In order to usher in the peace of God, we must remember to cooperate with the Holy Spirit by being obedient to the Word. We need to use our words to speak to the storm. We have to put a guard over our hearts and allow only peaceful words to come out of our mouths. As different conversations and situations arise in our daily lives, we need to be ever cognizant of the Greater One inside us and the fruit of peace. By choosing to speak only soft words, we'll turn away wrath. When we are faced with controversy, we study how to answer properly with the wisdom and peace of God. Finally, our words of peace can edify others, bring sweetness to the soul, and even healing to the body. That's the power of God's peace through the presence of the Holy Spirit in us!

STUDY QUESTIONS

Be diligent to present yourself approved to God, a worker
who does not need to be ashamed, rightly dividing the word of truth.
— 2 Timothy 2:15

1. Philippians 4:7 says, "And the peace of God, which surpasses all understanding, will guard your hearts and minds through Christ Jesus." In other words, God's peace can act as a guard over your heart and mind. Have you been allowing peace to guard your mouth and the words you speak?

2. The book of Proverbs has much to say about the power of our words. What verses from Proverbs have helped you speak words of peace in a situation?

3. Mark chapter 4 records the account of Jesus speaking peace to the storm. If you were one of His disciples on the boat, how do *you* think you would have reacted to the storm? What would have been your response to Jesus' command of peace?

PRACTICAL APPLICATION

But be doers of the word,
and not hearers only, deceiving yourselves.
— James 1:22

Learn to release God's peace into your words and conversations.

1. Take a moment to reflect on the words you usually use to speak with people. Are they words of peace or of conflict? Are you giving a soft answer that turns away wrath, or are you provoking anger through your choice of words and tone of voice?

2. When you encounter negative words from others like anger or gossip, how do you respond? Do you take a moment to think before you speak, or do you allow your feelings to dictate your words? How does the revelation of the fruit of peace help you put a guard over your mouth?

3. Have you ever experienced a moment of conflict with another person when you had to back away from the conversation to gather your

thoughts and calm your emotions? Did you ask the Holy Spirit to help you before re-engaging in the conversation?

TOPIC

Your Joy Is Loaded With Power

SCRIPTURES

1. **Psalm 118:24** — This is the day the Lord has made; We will rejoice and be glad in it.

2. **Zephaniah 3:17** — The Lord your God in your midst, the Mighty One, will save; He will rejoice over you with gladness, He will quiet you with His love, He will rejoice over you with singing.

3. Psalm 45:7 — You love righteousness and hate wickedness; therefore God, Your God, has anointed You with the oil of gladness more than Your companions.

4. **Hebrews 1:9** — You have loved righteousness and hated lawlessness; therefore God, Your God, has anointed You with the oil of gladness more than Your companions.

5. **Proverbs 17:22** — A merry heart does good, like medicine, but a broken spirit dries the bones.

6. **Philippians 4:4** — Rejoice in the Lord always. Again I will say, rejoice!

7. **1 Thessalonians 5:16** — Rejoice always.

SYNOPSIS

Not only is joy a fruit of the Spirit, but it is also a powerful expression of the Greater One living inside you. The Bible reveals different ways God Himself expresses joy. The New Testament provides examples of joyfulness from Jesus' earthly ministry. The apostle Paul also provided an excellent teaching from his own life on the importance of rejoicing during times of suffering. The joy of God is reflected through thankfulness, a merry heart, and joyful expressions. The joy that comes from inside a believer is supernatural, and it has the power to conquer every difficulty!

The emphasis of this lesson:

God's joy is so powerful that it can overcome depression, anger, anxiety, and any other negative emotion. As a born-again believer, you already have this joy present in you through the Holy Spirit. You can learn to discern how God's joy behaves in a variety of situations simply by studying the Bible. As you learn to cooperate with the joy of the Holy Spirit and release it by faith even during times of suffering and distress, you can rise above every challenge by the supernatural power of God.

The Power of God's Joy

As we continue our study on the Greater One, let's take a look at the powerful joy that the Holy Spirit brings into our lives. This kind of joy is greater than any depression, oppression, or problems that come against us. In fact, this joy is so powerful that it pushes all those things out of the way because it is a conquering joy.

Denise shared a personal testimony of how God's joy transformed her life. As a young girl, she had begun to develop a melancholy attitude, which affected her outlook on life as well as her relationships. At times she would be happy and outgoing, but at other times she would become melancholic, sad, and serious. Her behavior became so gloomy that when she would come to the breakfast table, her dad would say, "Well, here comes the bear!"

After a while, Denise began to realize that her moody attitude wasn't a blessing to anyone. The Lord brought correction and encouragement to her heart through His Word, reminding her that Psalm 118:24 says, "This is the day the Lord has made; we will rejoice and be glad in it." As she continued to meditate on that verse, Denise realized that rejoicing and being glad in the Lord wasn't a suggestion, but rather a clear, definite command from the Lord.

As a result of this revelation, Denise started changing her attitude. Instead of dragging herself into the kitchen with a sullen expression and pouty words, she decided to put on joy. When she woke up in the morning, she looked into the mirror and repeated to herself, "This is the day the Lord has made. I will rejoice and be glad in it!" She chose to be joyful the moment she got out of bed, and she carried that joy with her to the family breakfast table. Her obedience to the Word of God set her free from the doldrums, and she became a much more pleasant person to be around.

Characteristics of God's Joy

Because God's Word is a lamp unto our feet and a light unto our path (*see* Psalm 119:105), it shows us how we can operate in the fullness of joy. It reveals what specific attitudes and actions we need to take so we don't stifle the expression of the joy living inside us by the Holy Ghost. By spending time in God's Word, we can better discern how God's joy behaves and what makes His joy so different than the attitudes of the world.

A powerful scripture that describes the joy of God in action is Zephaniah 3:17: "The Lord your God in your midst, the Mighty One, will save; He will rejoice over you with gladness, He will quiet you with His love, He will rejoice over you with singing." God is not depressed! In fact, when He looks at you He sees Jesus on the inside of you. He views you as His treasure, His trophy of grace. Because the blood of Jesus has washed you clean, God rejoices over you!

The word "rejoice" in this passage actually means *to spin around*. It conveys the thought of God getting so excited about you that He just spins around with joy. He is thrilled over you as His child. This exuberant show of outward celebration is how God expresses His joy. Because we have the Greater One — the Holy Spirit — inside us, we can allow Him to express that kind of joy in us and through us anywhere we go.

Have you ever been around someone who exudes joy all the time? Their joy is contagious! Their delightful perspective, laughter, smile, and encouraging words inspire others and lift up their spirits. Why? Because joy is actually a presence. It conquers depression, fear, anxiety, and a host of other negative emotions. Joyfulness comes from the Holy Spirit inside us and it's greater than anything in the world.

God's joy is also revealed through the character of Jesus when He lived on this earth. He did not walk around grouchy, grumpy, angry, or depressed. Rather, He exhibited joy, love, kindness, and peace to all those around Him. Hebrews 1:9 tells us, "You have loved righteousness and hated lawlessness; therefore God, Your God, has anointed You with the oil of gladness more than Your companions." This verse is written in reference to Jesus, who had more joy than any of His companions.

Jesus' disciples weren't always perfect. In fact, they made mistakes and quarreled at times, but that didn't disturb Jesus' joy. He didn't let the actions of others bring Him down. While He corrected in love and firmness, He maintained a joyful attitude. He had conquering joy!

Jesus also had a lightheartedness about Him that kept Him anchored even during stressful situations. For example, after the resurrection, Mary was distraught thinking Jesus' body had been taken somewhere. When Jesus found her weeping, He simply asked, "Who are you looking for? Why are you crying?" Although this was a serious, powerful moment in history, Jesus stopped to talk to Mary and connected with her personally. Of course, He knew the reason why she was crying and carrying on in such an emotional way. But instead of scolding or chastising her, Jesus approached her in a loving, lighthearted manner. The power of the resurrection expressed itself in joy.

Whenever people around us are experiencing distressful situations, we can remember the joy and lightheartedness Jesus expressed to others. We don't have to become wrapped up in another person's anxiety or stress; instead, we can encourage them and lift up their spirits through joy. By releasing God's joyfulness from our hearts, we can bring joy and healing into any situation.

Conquering Joy

The joy of the Lord has the supernatural power to conquer anything that crosses its path including sickness and disease. The Bible says that a merry heart does good like a medicine (*see* Proverbs 17:22). Expressions of joy, such as laughter and singing, can act like medicine to our bodies, causing them to become stronger and healthier. Even medical science has proven that the healing process can be expedited through laughter and expressions of joy.

A person who is full of God's joy can also overcome times of suffering and distress. The apostle Paul showed this principle to be true when he wrote the book of Philippians during his years of imprisonment. Scholars agree that the Roman prisons during that era were terrible places full of sewage, rats, and the stench of death. Despite his squalid surroundings, Paul taught about joy and rejoicing all throughout his letter to the Philippian church. He wrote, "Rejoice in the Lord always. Again I will say, rejoice!" (Philippians 4:4)

If Paul was able to rejoice in such a wretched place of suffering, surely we, too, can acknowledge the Holy Spirit's presence of joy inside us during our own difficult circumstances. When joy comes forth in times of trouble, that is indeed supernatural! This kind of joy is so powerful that it conquers despair and changes circumstances.

Perhaps you may find it a challenge to rejoice at *all* times. A secret to keeping your joy stirred up, even during the worst of circumstances, is to practice thankfulness. Instead of complaining about the difficulties, learn to be grateful for even the smallest blessings in life. You can start off with the simple things that God has provided for you such as your home, food, family, and friends. After you go through the list of natural things in life you're thankful for, then you can stretch out a little further and begin thanking God for all the wonderful spiritual blessings He's given you: salvation, the hope of heaven, God's Word, and the Holy Spirit. By continually keeping your mind focused on what you *do* have as opposed to what you *do not* have, your joy will increase. Thanksgiving goes a long way in keeping your heart free of grief and sorrow, and it also stops you from becoming a person who complains all the time.

Expressing and living in joy is a choice you can make every day, no matter what situations may surround you. By acknowledging the Greater One inside you, you can tap into the joy that's already present in your spirit and release it anytime. The Holy Spirit in you is greater than anything that's coming against you in the world. He wants to express Himself through His joy in you at all times.

In sharing about the power of joy, Denise recalled an incident when she had to stir up her joy even though she wasn't feeling well in her body. Her mother had come to visit her in Latvia, and as they were walking in the town center, her mother asked her to start singing. At first, Denise was hesitant to do such a thing, especially since there were all kinds of people walking around the streets. However, since her mother continued to press the issue, she decided to put aside her feelings and start singing. Before too long, a crowd began gathering to listen. She quickly found herself enjoying the moment and taking pleasure in her mother's joy. After the impromptu concert, Denise realized she was no longer feeling ill, her headache had dissipated, and her joy returned. God's joy had healed her, energized her, and turned a challenging moment into one full of merriment.

If you're facing a challenging situation, sickness in your body, or a stressful time, you can rise above it through the power of God's joy inside you.

Perhaps you might not feel like expressing that joy, but you can do it by faith. You can say, "Depression, I'm done with you. I'm going to laugh, rejoice, and sing. This is the day the Lord has made, and I'm going to rejoice and be glad in it!"

By choosing to release the joy of the Holy Spirit, you can change the trajectory of your life and overcome the difficult days. Whenever times of suffering try to bring you down, you can think about Paul in that dark, stinky prison cell. If he could rejoice in the midst of squalor, so can you! Take a lesson from God Himself and spin around as an expression of joy and delight. Follow Jesus' example and learn to approach life with a light and joyful heart. Practice thankfulness even over the simplest blessings in life. Refuse to be a complainer, but instead, be an overflowing well of joy. And remember that God's Word says a cheerful heart is good medicine. The more you release the power of God's joy into your life, the higher you'll rise above every difficult place. You can be a conqueror and an overcomer just through the power of joy!

STUDY QUESTIONS

Be diligent to present yourself approved to God, a worker who does not need to be ashamed, rightly dividing the word of truth.
— 2 Timothy 2:15

1. The Bible teaches that God rejoices over you with joy. Have you ever considered the great joy God takes over His creation, which includes you?
2. Proverbs 17:22 tells us that a merry heart does good like a medicine. When was the last time you laughed during a time you didn't feel like laughing? How did expressing joy bring healing to you?
3. When Paul wrote his epistle to the Philippians, he was surrounded by the terrible stench and squalor of the Roman prison. Despite his living conditions, Paul continued to rejoice. Can you think of a time when you had to rejoice despite your environment? What happened when you chose to express the joy of the Holy Spirit inside you?

PRACTICAL APPLICATION

But be doers of the word,
and not hearers only, deceiving yourselves.
— James 1:22

Learn to express God's supernatural joy living inside you!

1. If you are dealing with any kind of health issue, how have you learned to express joy despite your tiredness or uncomfortableness? If you've been focusing more on how your body feels instead of expressing joy, how can you make that change today?

2. What are the simple joys in your life? What are your spiritual blessings that you're thankful for?

3. When you are around people, do you pull them up or down? Do you encourage others through words and expressions of joy and thanksgiving? Or do people run away from you because of your sour attitude?

LESSON 4

TOPIC

The Great-Tasting Fruit Inside You: Gentleness!

SCRIPTURES

1. **1 John 4:4** — You are of God, little children, and have overcome them, because He who is in you is greater than he who is in the world.

2. **Proverbs 3:1-8** — My son, do not forget my law, but let your heart keep my commands; For the length of days and long life and peace they will add to you. Let not mercy and truth forsake you; Bind them around your neck, write them on the tablet of your heart, and so find favor and high esteem in the sight of God and man. Trust in the Lord with all your heart, and lean not on your own understanding; In all your ways acknowledge Him, and He shall direct your paths. Do not be wise in your own eyes; Fear the Lord and depart from evil. It will be health to your flesh, and strength to your bones.

SYNOPSIS

Another way the Holy Spirit expresses Himself in us is through gentleness. This fruit of the Spirit is often made evident by our actions of mercy and truth. Proverbs chapter 3 reveals how mercy and truth can grow in our lives and what rewards can be harvested when we choose to acknowledge the Lord in all our ways.

The emphasis of this lesson:

As a born-again believer, you have the ability to walk in the power of gentleness. This quality is often expressed through mercy and truth operating in your life and relationships. By closely studying Proverbs 3, you can learn how to cultivate a fruitful life full of mercy and truth. In the end, a life that's consecrated to God reaps powerful rewards of health and peace.

The Power of God's Gentleness Expressed Through Mercy and Truth

Because of the indwelling presence of the Holy Spirit, we can walk in gentleness towards others. This gentleness is supernatural, and it is expressed through mercy and truth. By walking in the gentleness of God, our behavior, actions, and attitudes can be a blessing to those around us, even during times of disagreement or conflict.

Whenever we need wisdom to guide us, we can go to God's Word and discover the best way to respond in different situations. Since gentleness comes from God, His Word shows us how to display this character in our lives. Proverbs chapter 3 in particular reveals some wonderful truths regarding the expression of gentleness. Let's take a look at this passage verse by verse to uncover principles that will help us navigate difficult decisions and relationships.

This chapter starts off by saying, "My son, do not forget my law, but let your heart keep my commands; For the length of days and long life and peace they will add to you" (Proverbs 3:1-2). By keeping God's commands, the fruitfulness of our days will increase. Of course, this doesn't mean we'll have 27 hours in a day instead of 24. But by being obedient to the Word of God, we will be able to get more done in the allotted time. Little things won't steal our time because our hearts are centered on God's ways, His wisdom, and His attitudes.

The next verse says this: "Let not mercy and truth forsake you; Bind them around your neck, write them on the tablet of your heart" (v. 3). Sometimes mercy and truth have a way of trying to escape us! Instead of wanting to extend mercy, our flesh often wants to judge or criticize. But the Bible tells us to bind mercy and truth around our neck so they will always be evident in our actions towards others.

One way to extend mercy to others is to remember how merciful God has been towards you. Whenever you're tempted to pick up a stone and throw it at someone, you need to pause and reflect upon the times God has shown you mercy when you didn't do something right. His mercy was great towards you! With that attitude in mind, you can put down your stone, walk away from criticism, and show another person mercy just as God has shown you.

When it comes to living and speaking truth to others, you have to remember the truth of God's Word at all times. Circumstances don't change the Word because the Word is eternal. God's principles of truth don't change based on different situations or events. His truth is established and unchanging. So when something comes to steal truth from your heart or from the heart of another, remember that God's Word remains the same. Bind His truth around your neck so that you don't escape it.

Writing mercy and truth upon the tables of our hearts allows us to self-correct when we make mistakes. If we realize we've criticized another instead of showing mercy, that mercy written on our hearts will cause us to repent, turn around, apologize, and act in a merciful way. If we've not been walking in a truthful way, that truth will rise up from our hearts correcting our direction and redirecting our steps back to truthfulness.

There is nothing wrong with recognizing a mistake and backing up to make the correction. We are growing up in Christ, and self-correction is a part of the process. Like the apostle Paul wrote in Philippians 4:11, we must learn the art of being content in all things. It's easy sometimes to beat ourselves down when we miss it. Thankfully, we don't have to live in condemnation — we can simply go to God, repent for our wrongdoing, and correct what we've done. This is part of training ourselves in righteousness! Whenever we find mercy and truth escaping us, we can just say,

"No, you don't. You come back here. I'm going to show mercy. I'm going to walk in truth."

If we remain committed to God's process of growth in us, the Holy Spirit will show us how and when to self-correct when we miss it. He is our Helper, our Guide, our Comforter, and our Teacher. We would be so lost without Him! This is why it's so important to listen to those little nudges inside your heart — that's the Holy Spirit teaching you, correcting you, and guiding you into mercy and truth. If He says, "Don't say that," then learn to yield to His promptings. If He says, "Smile. I can handle this problem if you'll let Me," then put a grin on your face and release the care to the Lord.

Because the Holy Ghost inside you is greater than anything in the world, He can show you how to conquer whatever is coming against you or causing you to trip up. At times, you may hear the Holy Spirit speak to you, "Don't say that. Keep your mouth closed." When you hear and obey Him, you are acknowledging the Greater One inside you. That's how God's gentleness can be expressed in your life through mercy and truth.

When we choose to obey God and follow the way of mercy and truth, there are rewards that come our way. Proverbs 3:4 states, "And so find favor and high esteem in the sight of God and man." By disciplining ourselves to show mercy and truth, we will find favor and high esteem in the sight of God and man.

Trusting in the Lord

In our walk with the Lord, it's important to learn to trust Him to lead and guide us in all we say and do. Proverbs 3:5 says, "Trust in the Lord with all your heart, and lean not on your own understanding." Our flesh tends to treat others in certain ways or act judgmental or harsh. But when we place our trust in the Lord and listen to our heart, He will guide us into all truth and show us how we can express His gentleness in every situation. Trusting in Him is a safe place!

The Bible tells us we are not to lean on our own understanding. Our own thoughts and experiences may view certain situations or people in one way, but the Bible tells us we aren't to lean on our own thoughts or understanding. We are to put our full trust and confidence in Him and allow Him to lead us and guide us. By trusting in Him with our whole hearts, we won't be deceived into doing things just because someone else says we should do them. We're not moved by what others think or say about us because our trust is not in them — it's in the Lord.

When we trust God, we begin to experience His peace in our lives. We shut down all the other voices around us and hone in on the still, small voice speaking to us in our hearts. That's how the Holy Spirit leads us. He's the Greater One, and He will show us how to overcome any situation by expressing His gentleness, mercy, and truth.

Once we hear God's direction in our hearts, we have the full assurance that His answer is solid and trustworthy. Proverbs 3:6 says, "In all your ways acknowledge him, and he shall direct your paths." Acknowledging God in all our ways means yielding to Him in what we're about to say or what we're planning to do. He'll then show us the steps to take by giving us peace in the decision-making process. He'll direct our paths to things that please Him and bring glory to Jesus. He'll show us how to walk in the paths of righteousness, mercy, truth, and joy. He'll lead us into love, power, and soundness of mind.

By acknowledging Him in all our ways, we make room for Him in our lives, decisions, and relationships. He'll give us the right words to say at the right moment. We may not know what to do, but if we'll turn off our own ideas and listen to that still, small voice — the Greater One — inside us, He will give us the answer we need.

Leaning to our own understanding will lead us into things of the flesh. Instead of responding to situations in the peace, mercy, and truth of God, we'll react in unbecoming ways. For instance, there was a woman who was upset with her husband for watching TV all the time. So she decided to take things into our own hands and threw the TV out the window! But this didn't solve her problem — her husband went out and just bought another TV. Because that woman's actions were not led by the Spirit of God, she didn't act in a gentle way towards her husband. Instead, she brought additional strife into her home, and the problem just continued to worsen.

When we lean on our own understanding and try to do things the way we think we should do them, we put ourselves in danger of making foolish, unwise, and selfish decisions. This type of behavior doesn't bless others or solve problems; it just creates more hurt and confusion. However, if we're obedient to the Word and acknowledge God in all our ways, He will show us how to act and respond in every situation. Not only will relationships improve because of gentleness, mercy, and truth, but problems will be solved as well.

Our obedience to lean not on our own understanding will lead to great rewards. Proverbs 3:7-8 says, "Do not be wise in your own eyes; Fear the Lord and depart from evil. It will be health to your flesh, and strength to your bones" When we recognize our limitations and humble ourselves before the Lord, He will give us the answer to the problems we're facing. As a result, we will experience health and healing!

By acknowledging the Lord, we give up striving and come to a place of rest and trust in Him. All that emotional energy we spend trying to prove that our way is the correct way can lead to exhaustion, strife, mental fatigue, stress, and sickness. But the moment we acknowledge the Lord and turn things over to Him, He can lead us to a fresh and green pasture where peace, joy, and gentleness reside. By trusting in Him and walking in the fear of the Lord, we can enjoy a healthy life, loving relationships, and great joy in the journey.

As we walk through life recognizing the presence of the Holy Spirit inside us, our days will be filled with fruitfulness, longevity, and peace. We will have the wisdom to handle conflicts with gentleness. Mercy and truth won't escape us, but instead, will anchor our hearts. By acknowledging the Lord in every decision we make, we can stay away from wrong decisions and wrong paths. In the end, we'll enjoy health, peace, and provision simply because we chose to acknowledge the presence of the Greater One inside us!

STUDY QUESTIONS

Be diligent to present yourself approved to God, a worker who does not need to be ashamed, rightly dividing the word of truth.
— 2 Timothy 2:15

1. Proverbs 3:2 reminds us that obeying God leads to a fruitful, productive life. What difference can you see in your daily productivity when you remain steadfast in obedience to God?

2. Proverbs 3:3 teaches us not to let go of mercy and truth. Can you think of a time in your life when you didn't act in mercy? What was the outcome of that situation?

3. Proverbs 3:5 says to trust in the Lord with all your heart and not to lean on your own understanding. What has happened in your life as a result of trusting in God?

PRACTICAL APPLICATION

**But be doers of the word,
and not hearers only, deceiving yourselves.
—James 1:22**

Learn to acknowledge God in all your ways.

1. Do you start your day by acknowledging God? How does your productivity increase when you are cognizant of God's leading and presence in your daily life?

2. Have you been tempted to react to someone in criticism or judgment instead of mercy? What was the outcome of that situation? How was peace restored?

3. What are some of the ways you are tempted to act out from your own understanding? How can you reign in those reactions and replace them with trusting God for His guidance and wisdom?

LESSON 5

TOPIC

Yielding to God's High-Level Love

SCRIPTURES

1. **Romans 5:5** — Now hope does not disappoint, because the love of God has been poured out in our hearts by the Holy Spirit who was given to us.

2. **Matthew 5:43-46** — You have heard that it was said, 'You shall love your neighbor and hate your enemy.' But I say to you, love your enemies, bless those who curse you, do good to those who hate you, and pray for those who spitefully use you and persecute you, that you may be sons of your Father in heaven; for He makes His sun rise on the evil and on the good, and sends rain on the just and on the unjust. For

if you love those who love you, what reward have you? Do not even the tax collectors do the same?

3. **Philippians 4:7** — And the peace of God, which surpasses all understanding, will guard your hearts and minds through Christ Jesus.

4. **2 Corinthians 4:7** — But we have this treasure in earthen vessels, that the excellence of the power may be of God and not of us.

5. **Proverbs 15:1** — A soft answer turns away wrath, but a harsh word stirs up anger.

6. **Proverbs 16:32** — He who is slow to anger is better than the mighty, and he who rules his spirit than he who takes a city.

7. **Philippians 4:4** — Rejoice in the Lord always. Again I will say, rejoice!

SYNOPSIS

The Holy Spirit's presence in a believer is made evident through the expression of the fruit of the Spirit. This varied fruit is poured out into the heart at the new birth and includes love, peace, joy, and self-control. By learning to release these precious treasures, a believer is equipped to overcome any circumstance they may encounter.

The emphasis of this lesson:

When you received salvation, a precious treasure was deposited in you by the Holy Spirit. This treasure includes love, forgiveness, and peace. In this review lesson, you'll learn how to live a victorious life simply by releasing the power of God through the beautiful fruit of the Spirit.

A Summary of the Fruit of the Spirit

The Greater One living inside us produces beautiful fruit in our life. By acknowledging and releasing His power in us, we can display His lovely attributes for all to see. The fruitfulness of the Christian life isn't just for our own pleasure, but it also draws others to Christ. It allows them to taste and see that the Lord is good!

One of the most wonderful attributes the Holy Spirit produces is the love of God. Romans 5:5 says, "…The love of God has been poured out in our hearts by the Holy Spirit who was given to us." The moment you became born again is the moment when the Holy Spirit began pouring God's love into your heart. But this isn't the natural, emotion-driven human love — this is the highest quality of love that exists. It's the God kind of love, which is a high-level love!

God's love in you is capable of doing amazing things. You can love your enemies and bless those who curse you. You can do good to those who hate you and pray for your persecutors (*see* Matthew 5:43-46). Those actions aren't possible with just natural, human love. God's love far surpasses what only human love can accomplish because it is supernatural. And it resides in you by the Holy Ghost!

Forgiveness is another attribute of the Holy Spirit's presence in our lives. Although people may have done hurtful things to us in the past, we can forgive and release them by the power of God. The Bible teaches that because God has forgiven us, we can forgive others. We can reach down inside our hearts and pull up God's supernatural love that has been placed there by the Holy Spirit. From a natural standpoint, forgiveness may be difficult or even impossible. But God's love activated by the Holy Spirit can release forgiveness to anyone regardless of the pain that person may have caused.

Another beautiful fruit of the Holy Spirit is peace, which is something we all need — especially in these last days! Philippians 4:7 says, "And the peace of God, which surpasses all understanding, will guard your hearts and minds through Christ Jesus." The peace of God is so powerful that it can hold us in a steady place even when we don't understand it. It will stand at attention like a guard over our life protecting our heart and mind.

The Bible says that you have this treasure in an earthen vessel (*see* 2 Corinthians 4:7). You can feel pretty "earthy" when life is not going well or when things aren't going your way. Obstacles can discourage you and cause trouble. You may become tired, weary, or worn out from dealing with all the challenges. But that's when the Holy Spirit's power can take hold of you from the inside and help you overcome. You have this treasure in you — the Greater One — and all His perfect attributes.

To walk in peace properly, the Bible gives us some practical principles we can apply to our lives. Proverbs 15:1 reminds us that a soft answer turns away wrath. When we're tempted to reply to someone in an ugly way, we can just pull out that treasure that is within us and respond with a gentle answer. And Proverbs 15:28 says, "The heart of the righteous studies how to answer, but the mouth of the wicked pours forth evil." When we're relying on the Holy Spirit, He'll show us how to answer a situation appropriately with the wisdom of God. All of these practical applications from God's Word will help us retain peace in our relationships.

Another fruit of the Spirit is self-control. Proverbs 16:32 says, "He who is slow to anger is better than the mighty, and he who rules his spirit than he who takes a city." The Holy Spirit can help us control our mouth and our temper so that we don't hurt others or say things we shouldn't. Unfortunately, many homes, marriages, and relationships have been destroyed because people couldn't control themselves or their emotions. But if we'll choose to surrender to the working of the Holy Spirit inside us, we can use self-control. As a result, we can enjoy peaceful, healthy, and happy relationships with others.

Joy is another beautiful fruit of the Holy Spirit and is such a powerful force! Even the apostle Paul learned to rely on the fruit of joy when he was living in deplorable prison conditions. In fact, the whole book of Philippians was written to emphasize the power of rejoicing during times of suffering.

Releasing the fruit of the Spirit is a choice we are all responsible for in our lives. We can choose to live in bitterness, or we can choose to allow the fruit of love to dominate us. We can choose peace or fear; joy or sorrow; selfishness or self-control. By choosing to release the fruit of the Spirit, we are free to run and finish our race in complete victory.

You have a powerful treasure inside you — the Greater One and His wonderful, beautiful fruit that is already present in your spirit. It's up to you to acknowledge His presence and release His glorious treasure in your life. By allowing the Holy Spirit to express Himself in you through the fruit of the Spirit, you can overcome all!

STUDY QUESTIONS

> **Be diligent to present yourself approved to God, a worker**
> **who does not need to be ashamed, rightly dividing the word of truth.**
> **— 2 Timothy 2:15**

1. Matthew 4 teaches us how to love our enemies. Can you think of a time when you had to release God's love in you to a rival or enemy?

2. God's Word tells us to forgive others. Is there anyone in your life you've had trouble forgiving? Take a moment to release forgiveness from your heart towards that individual.

3. Proverbs 16:32 says, "He who is slow to anger is better than the mighty, and he who rules his spirit than he who takes a city." In what areas do you find it difficult to practice self-control? Will you determine to reach down inside your spirit and release self-control in that part of your life?

PRACTICAL APPLICATION

**But be doers of the word,
and not hearers only, deceiving yourselves.
—James 1:22**

Practice living in the fruit of the Spirit.

1. Of the different fruit of the Spirit mentioned in this chapter, with which ones do you have trouble, and with which ones do you excel?

2. Ask a friend or family member who knows you well if he or she sees evidence of the fruit of the Spirit in your life. His or her answer may surprise you!

3. Think of someone in your life who exemplifies Christ. What fruit of the Spirit is evident to you in that person?

Notes

CLAIM YOUR FREE RESOURCE!

As a way of introducing you further to the teaching ministry of Rick Renner, we would like to send you free of charge his teaching CD, "How To Receive a Miraculous Touch From God."

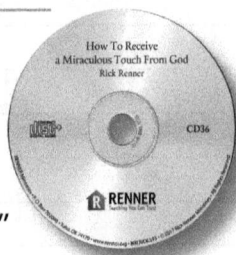

In His earthly ministry, Jesus commonly healed *all* who were sick of *all* their diseases. In this profound message, learn about the manifold dimensions of Christ's wisdom, goodness, power, and love toward all humanity who came to Him in faith with their needs.

☑ **YES, I want to receive Rick Renner's monthly teaching letter!**

Simply scan the QR code to claim this resource or go to:
renner.org/claim-your-free-offer

Connect

WITH US!

R renner.org   **f** facebook.com/rickrenner

▶ youtube.com/rennerministries   ◉ instagram.com/rickrrenner

www.ingramcontent.com/pod-product-compliance
Lightning Source LLC
Chambersburg PA
CBHW051050030426
42339CB00006B/293